UNCOLLECTED POEMS, DRAFTS, FRAGMENTS, & TRANSLATIONS

BOOKS BY GARY SNYDER

POETRY

Riprap and Cold Mountain Poems
Myths and Texts
The Back Country
Regarding Wave
Turtle Island
Axe Handles
Left Out in the Rain
No Nature
Mountains and Rivers Without End
Danger on Peaks
This Present Moment

PROSE

Earth House Hold
He Who Hunted Birds in His Father's Village
Songs for Gaia
The Real Work
Passage Through India
Good Wild Sacred
The Practice of the Wild
A Place in Space
The Gary Snyder Reader
Look Out: A Selection of Writings
Back on the Fire
The High Sierra of California (with Tom Killion)
Tamalpais Walking (with Tom Killion)
The Selected Letters of Allen Ginsberg and Gary Snyder
*Distant Neighbors: The Selected Letters of
Wendell Berry and Gary Snyder*
The Great Clod
Dooby Lane (with Peter Goin)

GARY SNYDER

UNCOLLECTED POEMS, DRAFTS, FRAGMENTS, & TRANSLATIONS

COUNTERPOINT
BERKELEY, CALIFORNIA

Copyright © 2022 by Gary Snyder

All rights reserved
First Counterpoint edition: 2022

Counterpoint is happy to acknowledge The Library of America and
is grateful for their cooperation in the publication of this collection.

ISBN: 978-1-64009-577-9

The Library of Congress Cataloging-in-Publication data is available.

Jacket design by Nicole Caputo
Jacket calligraphy by Mary Teichman

COUNTERPOINT
2560 Ninth Street, Suite 318
Berkeley, CA 94710
www.counterpointpress.com

Printed in the United States of America

1 3 5 7 9 10 8 6 4 2

Contents

Editorial Note

As we began assembling the Gary Snyder volume for Library of America, we realized there were poems and translations central to Snyder's work that had not been collected into his previous books. As our pile grew, with Snyder's help and our further searches, the group became a significant collection, one we're happy to see into print as a separate publication. The text is drawn from #357 in The Library of America series, *Gary Snyder: Collected Poems*. Counterpoint is grateful for the cooperation of the Library of America and their wonderful professionals, especially including Max Rudin, Trish Hoard, Matthew Parr, and Brian McCarthy.

—Jack Shoemaker and Anthony Hunt

UNCOLLECTED POEMS, DRAFTS, FRAGMENTS, & TRANSLATIONS

a poem

walking lonely on a fall day
in a long meadow, slanting open to the woods
where the frost chilled
the dead grass, a year ago.

peer sharply through the brown grass:
the slim thin white thing rotted
long ago.

build now a squat stone tablet
for ants to sun on
and hide it in the dead grass:
"Here Lie My Children."

The Death of Rhea

"Behold, behold!" the Bowman said
With a fearful falling cry
While the man in black
With his blue jowls slack
Like a fluttering moth came wheeling back
From the pitiless velvet sky.

An Autumn Poem

This distraught season
Sunlight shivers on the grass
Like a pale genius in his bathrobe
Barefoot, wavering up the stairs.

All the lovely vicious women
Seeking Orpheus through the halls,
The poet cowering in the Men's Room:
A dead leaf, withered.

See his veins,
O Daughters of Jerusalem.

Kasina Song

Dallying in pleasant verdure
One warm Monday afternoon
Forming circles in the sand
With wet red clay, you cried,
"Insatiable are the lusts!"
A vision then appeared.

So I departed, bowl in hand
To live in this transcendent land.

"Escaping Cambridge"

Escaping Cambridge,
He turned away from London
With austere passion faced the seas

Accompanied by numbered boxes
Crossed the plains in teeming summer
Soft eyes avoiding sores and hunger

Stood sorrowful in cool Darjeeling:
Above the tea-brush Kanchenjunga falls unfurled
Placenta of the soil created
Strewn beyond Cathay

Through rank valleys, thirsty plains
Rising early—frost chilling sandalled feet—
Sleepy men muttering in an unknown tongue
Pack loaded, far from villages
So he could venture

Indus, Brahmaputra, silver shreds at glacier snout
Wheels of fluttering paper creaking turn

He fell beyond the mists of Chomolungma
Where even nomads shun to die
        Who is to say that demons did not kill him
Far from Tea and Cambridge?

1950–51

"Dear Mr. President"

Dear Mr. President:

There is no bomb in Gilead.
The red Chinese are not red Indians:
You could have saved the Sioux.
Please stop them building roads
In the North Cascades.

There were great white birds
In the tops of the banyan trees
Calling across the town,
When I was in Saigon.

       Respectfully yours,
       Gary Snyder

                       c. 1955

Hymn to the Goddess San Francisco in Paradise
If you want to live high get high—Nihil C.

I

up under the bell skirt
caving over the soil
white legs flashing
    —amazed to see under their clothes they are
                    naked
    this makes them sacred
& more than they are in their own shape
        free.

the wildest cock-blowing
      gang-fucking foul-tongued
         head chick
     thus the most so—

II

high town
high   in the dark   town
     dream   sex   church
     YAHWEH   peyote spook
     Mary the fish-eyed
         spotless,
         lascivious,
vomiting molten gold.

san fran sisco
hung over & swing down
         dancers on water
    oil slick glide
    shaman longshoremen
    magical strikes—
howls of the guardians rise from the waterfront.

—state line beauties those switcher engines
      leading waggons
warehouz of jewels and fresh fur

car leans
      on its downhill springs
            parked on mountainsides.
white minarets in the night
      demon fog chaos.
bison stroll on the grass.
       languid and elegant, fucking while standing
          young couples in silk
             make-up on.

crystal towers   gleam for a hundred miles
      poison oak hedges, walld child garden
& the ring mountains holding a cool
      basin of pure evening fog
      strained thru the bridge
      gold and orange,
beams of cars wiser than drivers
stream across promenades, causeways
      incensed exhaust.

smiling the City Hall Altar to Heaven
      they serve up the cock   tail,
there is higher than nature in city
         it spins in the sky.

III

quenching the blue flame
tasting the tea brought from China
cracking the fresh duck egg on white plate

passed out the gates of our chambers
over the clear miles, ships.
forever such ecstasy
      wealth & such beauty
      we live in the sign of Good Will . . .

(the white-robed saint trim my locks for
        a paltry sum . . . life is
        like free)
rolling lawns clippt and the smell of gum tree.
boiled crab from a saltwater vat.
                        rhine wine.
bison and elk of Chrysopylae
eels in those rocks in the wave
olive oil, garlic, soy, hard cheese.

Devas of small merit in Jambudvipa
Plucking sour berries to eat:
shall ascend to an eminence,
scanning the scene
                fog in
        from the Farallones
long ship low   far below
        sliding under the bridge
        bright white   red-lead.
                        —blue of the sea.
        on that ship is me.

                        IV
—smilers all on the nod nap on cots
but the slither   & breakfree
        tosst slipper up on the toe
            & the white thighs open
                the flesh of the wet flower
                        LAW
crossed eyes gleam   *come*
        flowery prints and
        yellow kettles in a row
        breast weight swelld down

kind chairmen smile around.
generals and presidents swallow
                hoping   they too   can come . . .
        THERE IS NO WAY

                        9

turn back dead tourist
drop your crumb your funny passport
—fall back richer spenders
think you make with wild teenager
on hard forever
crust in jewel
—*you are too old*.
the san francisco fake front strip tease
phony, sweaty,
last a minute and they stink and die

THIS LAND IS FOR THE HIGH
& love is for ten thousand years.
(damnd square climbers give me pains)
them wilty blossoms on her sweaty brow—
the flute and lute and drums

policecars sireen down on Fillmore
fog clears back away
the police close in
& shoot the loose
& clouds are slipping by

& hide it in your pockets.

It all becomes plain sky.

1965

The Elwha River

I was a girl waiting by the roadside for my boyfriend to come in his car.
I was pregnant, I should have been going to high school. I walked up
the road when he didn't come, over a bridge; I saw a sleeping man. I
came to the Elwha River—grade school—classes—I went and sat down
with the children. The teacher was young and sad-looking, homely; she
assigned us an essay:
"What I Just Did."

"I was waiting for my boyfriend by the Elwha bridge. The bridge was
redwood, a fresh bridge with inner bark still clinging on some logs—it
smelled good. There was a man there sleeping under redwood trees.
He had a box of flies by his head; he was on the ground. I crossed the
Elwha River by a meadow; it had a flat stony prong between two river
forks . . ."

Thinking this would please the teacher. We handed all the papers in, and
got them back—mine was C minus. The children then went home, the
teacher came to me and said
"I don't like you."
"Why?"
—Because I used to be a whore."

The Elwha River, I explained, is a real river, but not the river I
described. Where I had just walked was real but for the dream river—
actually the Elwha doesn't fork at that point.

As I write this I must remind myself that there is another Elwha, the
actual Olympic peninsula river, which is not the river I took pains to
recollect as real in the dream.

There are no redwoods north of southern
Curry County, Oregon.

21.X.1958

II

Marble hollow-ground hunting knife;

pigleather tobacco pouch
left on the ground at Whiskey Bend along
the Elwha, 1950—

Sewing kit. Blown off the cot beside me
on the boatdeck by a sudden wind
South China Sea;

A black beret Joanne had given me for my birthday
left in some
Kawaramachi bar.

Swiss army knife stole from my pants
at Juhu Beach outside Bombay,
a fine italic pen,

Theodora, Kitty-chan,
bottle of wine got broke.
things left on the sand.

Lost things.

III

Elwha, from its source. Threadwhite falls
out of snow-tunnel mouths with
cold mist-breath
saddles of deep snow on the ridges—

o wise stream—o living flow
o milky confluence, bank cutter
alder toppler
make meander
swampy acres   elk churned mud

The big Douglas fir in this valley.
Nobly groovd bark, it adapts: where Sitka spruce
cannot.
          Redwood and sequoia
resisting and enduring, as against adaptation;
one mind.

          Trail crew foreman says they finally got wise
to making trails low on the outside, so water
can run off good—before they were worried because
packstock always walks the outside of the trail
because they don't want to bump their loads on rocks
or trees   "punching out all the way from N Fork
over Low Divide & clear back here, this punchin gets
mighty old"

Puncheon slab saw cut *wowed*

"They got rip-cut chains now maybe different rakers
          this here punchin gets old"

          About 12:30 come to Whiskey Bend.
          That lowland smell.

                                        21.VIII.1964

A Lion Dream

I

Dressed up in slacks & good shoes I was going walking with two friends along a road a ways above a river. To get down, we found an opening in the bushes and a stairway made of stone. Slippery and some parts muddy, thick with moss. Down by the river I went out on a gravel-bar and looking back, I saw a lion coming up behind my friends. I shouted out a warning, and then waded in the river, thinking lions wouldn't swim. Clothes and all. I started swimming at an angle to the current—a fast, fairly shallow mountain river—

The lion started swimming too. Scrambling up the far bank, I threw rocks at the lion; one hit it on the nose. It changed into a girl. I kept on throwing rocks and she turned over in the water, one glancing off her belly. I ran to a house on the riverbank and rang the doorbell, getting scared. It sounded like the people in the house were trying to open up the door but it was stuck.

The Lion-girl was standing in the water wading out of the shallows. She was very young and slender; very high, very small, breasts; and no pubic hair. She was carrying a book. She came up on the porch and said "I live here." I said,
"You ought to let the neighbors know."

HAIL

to the Goddess in the LION FORM
     who swims rivers
high-breasted, slender,
     no body hair.

SHE who carries a book and
DWELLS
     on the opposite shore,

     svāhā

1967

A Curse
on the Men in Washington, Pentagon

OM A KA CA ṬA PA YA ŚA   SVĀHĀ

As you shoot down the Vietnamese girls and men
         in their fields
           burning and chopping,
           poisoning and blighting,

So surely I hunt the white man down
         in my heart.
The crew-cutted Seattle boy
The Portland boy who worked for U.P.
                that was me.

I won't let him live. The 'American'
         I'll destroy. The 'Christian'
              has long been dead.

They won't pass on to my children.
I'll give them Chief Joseph, the Bison herds,
Ishi, sparrowhawk, the Fir trees
The Buddha, their own naked bodies,
Swimming and dancing and singing
                instead.

As I kill the white man,
        the 'American'
        in me
And dance out the Ghost dance:
To bring back America, the grass and the streams,

To trample your throat in your dreams.

This magic I work, this loving I give
    that my children may flourish

And yours won't thrive.

HI'NISWA' VITA'KI'NI

June 1967

Smokey the Bear Sutra

Once in the Jurassic, about 150 million years ago,
the Great Sun Buddha in this corner of the Infinite
Void gave a great Discourse to all the assembled elements
and energies: to the standing beings, the walking beings,
the flying beings, and the sitting beings—even grasses,
to the number of thirteen billion, each one born from a
seed, were assembled there: a Discourse concerning
Enlightenment on the planet Earth.

"In some future time, there will be a continent called
America. It will have great centers of power called
such as Pyramid Lake, Walden Pond, Mt. Rainier, Big Sur,
Everglades, and so forth; and powerful nerves and channels
such as Columbia River, Mississippi River, and Grand Canyon.
The human race in that era will get into troubles all over
its head, and practically wreck everything in spite of
its own strong intelligent Buddha-nature."

"The twisting strata of the great mountains and the pulsings
of great volcanoes are my love burning deep in the earth.
My obstinate compassion is schist and basalt and
granite, to be mountains, to bring down the rain. In that
future American Era I shall enter a new form: to cure
the world of loveless knowledge that seeks with blind hunger;
and mindless rage eating food that will not fill it."

And he showed himself in his true form of

SMOKEY THE BEAR

A handsome smokey-colored brown bear standing on his
hind legs, showing that he is aroused and watchful.

18

Bearing in his right paw the Shovel that digs to the
truth beneath appearances; cuts the roots of useless attach-
ments, and flings damp sand on the fires of greed and war;

His left paw in the Mudra of Comradely Display—indicating
that all creatures have the full right to live to their limits
and that deer, rabbits, chipmunks, snakes, dandelions,
and lizards all grow in the realm of the Dharma;

Wearing the blue work overalls symbolic of slaves and
laborers, the countless men oppressed by a civilization
that claims to save but only destroys;

Wearing the broad-brimmed hat of the West, symbolic of
the forces that guard the Wilderness, which is the Natural
State of the Dharma and the True Path of man on earth;
all true paths lead through mountains—

With a halo of smoke and flame behind, the forest fires
of the kali-yuga, fires caused by the stupidity of those
who think things can be gained and lost whereas in truth all
is contained vast and free in the Blue Sky and Green Earth
of One Mind;

Round-bellied to show his kind nature and that the great
earth has food enough for everyone who loves her and trusts
her;

Trampling underfoot wasteful freeways and needless
suburbs; smashing the worms of capitalism and totalitarianism;

Indicating the Task: his followers, becoming free of cars,
houses, canned foods, universities, and shoes, master the
Three Mysteries of their own Body, Speech, and Mind; and
fearlessly chop down the rotten trees and prune out the
sick limbs of this country America and then burn the leftover
trash.

Wrathful but Calm, Austere but Comic, Smokey the Bear will Illuminate those who would help him; but for those who would hinder or slander him,

HE WILL PUT THEM OUT.

Thus his great Mantra:
Namah samanta vajranam chanda maharoshana
Sphataya hum traka ham mam

"I DEDICATE MYSELF TO THE UNIVERSAL DIAMOND
BE THIS RAGING FURY DESTROYED"

And he will protect those who love woods and rivers,
Gods and animals, hobos and madmen, prisoners and sick
people, musicians, playful women, and hopeful children;

And if anyone is threatened by advertising, air pollution,
or the police, they should chant SMOKEY THE BEAR'S WAR SPELL:

DROWN THEIR BUTTS
CRUSH THEIR BUTTS
DROWN THEIR BUTTS
CRUSH THEIR BUTTS

And SMOKEY THE BEAR will surely appear to put the enemy out
with his vajra-shovel.

Now those who recite this Sutra and then try to put it in
        practice will accumulate merit as countless as the sands
        of Arizona and Nevada,
Will help save the planet Earth from total oil slick,
Will enter the age of harmony of man and nature,
Will win the tender love and caresses of men, women, and beasts,
Will always have ripe blackberries to eat and a sunny spot under a pine
        tree to sit at.

AND IN THE END WILL WIN HIGHEST PERFECT
ENLIGHTENMENT.

thus have we heard.

(may be reproduced free forever)

February 1968

Kumarajiva's Mother
From Mountains & Rivers

Who was Kumarajiva's mother.
        giva-giva
        jiva-jiva   "some mysterious bird
with a lovely call. It has a human face
and two heads—a bird's body—"

        princess of the royal line of Kucha

"I don't know anything about it.   So I can't."
"I never met the lady . . . I don't know—I remember
       you telling a story about him the other day."

       she had freckles. she
       became a nun? She took him to Kashmir
       they met an arhat with a piercing glance

What do you mean by that?
       year by year his Chinese prose style grew—

"first great revolutionist in prose the next is
       Mao Tse-tung"

       he ate needles
       in China
       in front of all the monks, ah,
he liked girls.
       save innumerable people a scholar-master
              brilliant talent
         his mother?

Kumari
a girl about twelve
          "the girl without corsets
          "the lady of the mammoth

          Lakshmi is still riding elephants

She was a Kumari virgin.
A virgin of 11–12—or 13 "north Indian
          tantric gambit
     again a variation"

Did she *produce* him?
"She gave him the insight:
But not the consciousness
          of the Mother:
     she's sprinkling water
     into his eyes"

Nobody has ever lifted my veil

     The Mother . . . that's all.
     Nothing more about her.
     She was great, wasn't she,
     the sister of the emperor
     Her name was *Giva*.

                              1969

Song to the Raw Material

"I am one with my food"
          eskimo dreaming of the game
          they've killed,
    afraid it don't want to be reborn
    in edible form no more—

production, distribution, consumption.
the meat body's "changing   body"—

space is fucking with time on the
          edge   of things!

              meta-ecology or meta-economics

society / economics / politics / fucking
the meat—"changing body"—but fucking
crosses up all the lines:

          a process ticked off.

chewing peanuts.

April 1970

Down

Back to where it started.
Over the fields, looks level,
Begins to go down.
Thicker trees in this shade
A few ranches on benches
                          what river? valley
Lower, shadier, the trail less worn,
Rougher gulch,
Rockier, brushier,
Opening out on bare stone hogsback
                  arching bull hump forward
                  over and tilting, opening,
                  gorge,
Switchbacking down to that edge and around it,
Steeper, darker,
Cliffs breaking *under*,   closer,
A cool   a well
                of nothing
                happening beneath,   and to the lips
                there's no   stream
                             there
It keeps going:
                old tree trunk ladders,
                rusty iron stakes
                driven into cracks,   descending.
A rock falls.
Wind blowing softly *up*

I swallow, lean forward, look down:
My balls and belly turn over

        can   I   make   it?

It pulls—I hold—I hang *on*

Freezing—the chill—the pulse roar in the skull

      ah, gone   off

BLACK   TANGLE   MOTHER   EAGLE

      ah   bottomless blessing, gulping

        FALL

beyond   behind beyond   below beyond

EMPTY   BELLY   VOMIT   MUSIC   WHIRLING

        stars!

                         Fall 1970

Swimming Naked in the Yuba River

White, shining, boulders in the sun.
Light and water
Gathered in the gorge,
The world
In every grain of sand.
To step into this flowing
With a suit on
Would be a sin.

1971

The California Water Plan

Thunderstorm downpours on 395—south of Bridgeport—
and looking down into Mono Lake,
crackling
that fiery spirit, dark fist mudras
                                 two crossed fists
lightning jagged lines.

                  in man too, no purpose
                  but dark playful power.

Up the sandy trail   in a sacred way we come
Up the sandy trail   in a sacred way we come

creeks rush down through banks of flowers
          wild onions   lupines

               inbreath   hold   the snow
               outbreath, summer, let   them go

               middle fork, south fork, the san joaquin

Lined with flowers, the waters dancing gaily down;
the lacy leaves all wave goodbye! cascading toward
the gorges
cutting through the snake-dry foothills,
out into diversion ditches of the
tractor plains—

          sPhat!

           ACHALA
          "Immovable"

or Caṇḍamahāroṣaṇa "Lord of Heat"

color—yellow arms—two tools—sword and noose

"Four Sādhanas are devoted to his worship and he is always represented in yab-yum. The worshipper should think of himself as Caṇḍamahāroṣaṇa, whose color is like that of the Atasī flower and whose second name is Achala. He is one-faced, two-armed, and is squint-eyed. His face appears terrible with bare fangs. He wears a jeweled head-dress, bites his lips, and wears on his crown a garland of severed heads. His eyes are slightly red, and he carries the sword in his right hand and the noose round the raised index finger against the chest in the left. His sacred thread consists of a white snake; he is clad in tiger-skin and he wears jewels. He is radiant as the sun and bears on his crown the effigy of Akṣobhya. Thus he should be meditated upon. His worship is performed in secret . . ."
Benoytosh Bhattacharyya, *The Indian Buddhist Iconography*
   "Mainly based on the Sādhanamālā and cognate
   Tantric Texts of Rituals"

In this iconography he is considered an "emanation" of Akṣobhya, who is one of the five "Victors" or "Vectors" . . . one of the "five cosmic rays of evolution" . . . in the Vajradhātu Maṇḍala (Diagram of the Irreducible Space) Akṣobhya is green and maintains the East.

In Japan, where Achala is called Fudo, he is considered a direct emanation of Vairocana, the Great Sun Buddha, who is at the center of the five-spot mandala, the Unconditioned Body-of-Dharma represented, amazingly, WITH form, as "Lord of Forms" and in human form, Fudo statues to be found in cliffs, on peaks, by waterfalls, in mossy grottos and everywhere that rock crops out.
He stands in a halo of raging flame, or sits, his vehicle is rough rock, maybe half-molten magma. Thus he rides out wrath, and like a craggy peak his lover is Kwannon, the creeks that flow and keep back "nothing" til they "empty" in the sea.

ALL HAIL THE NOBLE UPLIFT OF THE JURASSIC
  CALLED SIERRA GRANITE

AND THOSE SINUOUS CLEFTS AND WINDING
WATERS THE DAKINIS WHO FLY IN SWIRLING
CLOUD MIST BRIGHTNESS

THOSE GODDESSES CALLED YUBA, BEAR AND
FEATHER, FIERY FIST AND THEIR GENTLE
DOWNHILL GLIDING BE ONE GIFT TO ALL

     & death to all dams.

November 1971

Greasy Boy

Dirt & tatters—dirt rubs off.
            rags, rags, rags
        tear it up
            tear it up
                over and over—
dirt, rags—tatters
the sand blown grim soot
                caking under eyes

Tear it up,
dirt and rags,
        —tattered—

Let them fly, dirt bits—down the wind.

across scab land.

I, I,
for "one"
        —not afraid of
dirt, and,
ragged,
me——death.

June 1973

"I saw the Mother once"

I saw the Mother once
at Pondicherry, morning darshan, looking up
til our necks were stiff, as she stared down at the little crowd
dawn street, with a fixed hypnotic smile and painted eyes,
finally backing off the balcony away.
Last night I dreamed again: the Mother
in her room upstairs, sitting on a concrete floor
her legs stuck out in front
like proper Navajo women used to do,
no cushion, someone said,   "The Mother."
I went forward and bowed low,
as I was once taught long ago
put my forehead to the floor.
She rubbed my ears,
stroked the neck, and said
. . . .
. . . .
. . . .
I forget.
& then showed me a letter which I read,
one side of the page about myself.
I think it said, "keep calm."
And the other side was all about my wife.
Much about Masa
. . . .
. . . .
. . . . and,
finally,
"dark powers."

June 1973

Tomorrow's Song

in the service
of the wilderness
of life
of death
of the Mother's breasts!
in the service
of the wilderness
of life
of Death
of the Mother's breaths!

Spring 1974

Gold, Green

Let it be
On a day in March
California;
When the grass is green
On the rolling hills
And the snow
Is deep in the mountains—

Let it be
On a day like this
That we plant a tree
California
For the years to come
For the little ones
And the lakes
Will be pure in the mountains—

Let it be gold and green
California;
That we touch the ground
That we heal the land
From the mountains to the sea.

c. March 1978

34

"The delicacy of the mountains"

The delicacy of the mountains
    "you lead me into dry pasture
    I eat thistle"

The art of maintenance,
ends curled back
              toward home
  passing through.

  balance of power,

  O Father Sun

                         1979

"Emptiness, anti-entropy ultimate"

Emptiness, anti-entropy ultimate

no friction whatever.

let it all slide.

The holy, the perfect, transcendent,

"grease"

1979

"The dried out winter ricefields"

The dried out winter ricefields
men far off loading junks in the river
bales of rice on their shoulders
a little boat poles out
      —roosters and geese—
     –looking at China

1983

"At Sarnath"

At Sarnath
    a Rongbuk, and a
twisty-horned white-bellied
        antelope, some
        elk and deer
            behind barbed wire.
a Lama tries
to sell Tibetan coin
the Grove where Buddha spoke.

1983

haiku

baby monkey taking first steps
   top of the wall
back of the tourist bungalow.

the tonga-wallah   (ponycart driver)
pinches the scab on his
        pony's haunch
instead of the whip

a sikh boy
like a wild little girl
   combs his long hair

monkeys wrestle
      in the thorny tree

on top of vulture peak
  nobody all morning
selling flowers.

      scrub jungle and monkeys,
      Rajagriha

barefeet on cold marble
  naked Jain genitals   (Sarnath)
    in the shadows.

letting tourists off his back
the painted elephant craps   (Amber)

lady in a nice sari
    walks quickly, not looking too much
at Khajuraho

1983

on the train

Sikhs and Punjabis
tired of looking at Joanne
        put their heads
between their knees
            and sleep.

1983

"nothing at the center"

nothing at the center
a huge old tree lives
spring by spring

1984

Needles Country of the Canyonlands

Down I-15 to Spanish Fork, thence Soldier Pass—Green River—Moab.
Turn off into Needles district of the Canyonlands. Camp at Squaw Flat.
Wine, crackers, up on the butte; almost half moon. Scramble down to
sleep at the foot of the rock under a juniper.

Saturday

  Walk over Butte 1, across a flat, into a canyon and over slickrock,
from the crest the wall of needles. Northerly around some ends—across
a small flat, and a pass, notch, defile. Lunch on a ledge through a gap
looking down. ["woven bamboo burden basket"]—descend into Ele-
phant Canyon and across, up, through a low pass, into   Chesler park.
                              camp in a cove
on a soil-building ledge.
Wingate—Navajo –Chinle formations. Ages of sand. What were the par-
ent materials? Sandstone locks in much of the world's oxygen.   Layers.
Soft parts under wear back leaving hard upper over-hanging. Layers laid
bare.   —Packed all our water in. Then, Saturday afternoon, explore out
the S. end through a gap, down into "joint canyon" a walk in vertical-
walled slots stemmed into—what echo—not echo, but reverberation,
muffled and low. *Gaté gaté paragaté parusamgaté   svāhā.*

Come down on sandy wash-bottom (used as a jeeproad) and rest with
Tom Dickman under a giant elderly Juniper. Return to camp to cook
and drink.

Sunday

(Gale Dick my companion speaks of his early college days—drive to grasp, master, the scientific view of the universe—what is it, "views of the universe" and our efforts to master them—the men in the kiva.)
   —to master "cultural lore"
   —via that, mastering as aspect of inborn
   psychological structuring, both individual and universal
   —via both above, master natural world fact &
   process.   Three overlapping questions. The
last phase having almost always been done through myth, a point of "view"
                    leaving us with that question, is any view not just a view & objectivity another variety of myth.

   wake to morning of snow. the firewood floating in a stream.   —from dry twigs under Juniper make a fire in tree-shelter on the kicked-out sand. Tea and *familia*—wet legs.
Then   down a direct way into Elephant Canyon—stash the packs—go upstream.
   (and quite suddenly streamwater starts running—comes rushing down, not rushing but rustling along, filling each pool then spilling onward—)
   Up on a ledge overlooking Druid Arch. Hailstorm while drifting sheets blow in swiftly as we race for shelter in an alcove overhang. Eat lunch, then step out into sunshine, of the arch, like a complex part of some machine, or set of inner earbones.

                    no route

        to the summit cap.
           remembering: roughly:

   & Back down E. Canyon skipping side-to-side; mushy sand steps mixed with rock slab or loose sub-surface boulder; but never a   slip— duck under Juniper limb—(sometimes by the trail *Mahonia fremontii* [who later discovered re-named *Berberis* . . .]) and retrieving packs proceed downstream to the squaw flat trail.   a yellow flower / paint-brush / a lupine / in bloom

[to master so much of the world.]

—So then, returning, sun-and-cloud—and long views over "Ernie's country" crosst the Colorado; and up there, THE MAZE. Such land. A dream of mudpies, sandboxes, slapped, whopped, dried out, hosed down, scuffed, leaving tricky runs of structures; following hard—and soft—the blow and flow of wind-and-water; years
    (seconds?) gone by, in which we wander like tentative exploring ants. What of this do the petroglyphs say, those ants who rambled here before.
    The long distant front of layered cliff.   Surface: this is where it's at now; but cut crosswise, the cliff, "This is what we've done."
    Back over the humps, benches, slots, and flats, to the car.
    A fenced-off tumble of logs near the car is an oldstyle Diné hogan ruin; I presume.
    In cloud and blue sky.   Rainpools, glittering on the rocks, wind whipping at the top of every rise.   Soft reddish sand, in every place that's dished and low.

the last weekend in March, '74

Spring 1990

45

from *"A Single Breath"*

Teasing the demonic
Wrestling the wrathful
Laughing with the lustful
Seducing the shy
Wiping dirty noses and sewing torn shirts
Sending philosophers home to their wives in time for dinner
Dousing bureaucrats in rivers
Taking mothers mountain climbing
Eating the ordinary

1991

from *"Coming into the Watershed"*

California is gold-tan grasses, silver-gray tule fog,
olive-green redwood, blue-gray chaparral,
silver-hue serpentine hills.
Blinding white granite,
blue-black rock sea cliffs.
—Blue summer sky, chestnut brown slough water,
steep purple city streets—hot cream towns.
Many colors of the land, many colors of the skin.

March 1–2, 1992

47

Ravynes Fly East

A volcano erupting under the sea
  becomes quartz porphyry

Hundreds of millions of years
  makes a peak

In a place of snow
  and careen of birds

Black, not vultures,
  croak and their tail-

Feathers swoop back upwards
  ten thousand feet

Ravens! a gang
  tangling, tumbling, rising

Then shoot up past us
  (shivering on the summit)

Eastward toward the desert,
  dots sailing off away.

Spring 1994

Daconstruction

They're slogging through the worksite,
rubber boots, pumps running, foot-wide hose
gushing steely water in a frothy pond

the link-belt crane turns like a Nō stage dance
dangles a trembling sixty-foot pipe.
Young guys in hardhat and T-shirts
hand-signal as it swings

To lower it tenderly
into a three-foot-wide casing
—a whomping cement truck backs in and
dumps down the pipe.

Eight at night—job lights glaring—
shrieks and whistles—
soupy mudponds—rebar and wire snipper trash
a high-rise building start
chain-linked off from the gridlocked streets,

another "economic miracle" of Asia,
smoking cigarettes and shouting—
laying new horizons on old swampy soils,
long-lost wetlands,
rainy noisy sticky city night,

Taipei.

Autumn 1994

49

Mountains Walk on Water

Sunrise a rose-red crack below the clouds, above the fog;
    folds of ranges north   edges burning

Shadow hollows, dropt-out dewy rounded cliffs,
    layer on layer—rock, cloud—

Snaky ridges wriggle the abyss   mountain wall mist tatters,
cloud veil thins and peels,
    a rush of water running down there rising—

Rose light leaping hill to hill—dark down gorges have no
end;

      no bottom to the bottom.

Taiwan's twenty million people
live below these mountain depths,

soaking cliffs and drippy elder trees.

c. 1995

from *"Allen Ginsberg Crosses Over"*

Cherry blossoms falling
    Young girls rising
        Us on the deck.

—

Raw tuna, saké,
    And blossoms.
        Spilled shoyu.

—

READING BASHŌ ON THE PLANE

Between lectures,
    This little seat by the window
        My hermitage.

1997

from *"The Cottonwoods"*

Deaf Smith. I remember that   *wheat*
    back in the sixties   drive out to the co-op for it
"Deef Smith County whole wheat berries"

                    and grind it ourselves.

Fall 1998

Where the Sammamish, the Snohomish, and the Skykomish All Come In

The sweet insipid taste of *salal*
and the sharp sour Oregon grape

bland salmonberry
spit-bugs inside

grasshoppers under dry
cowpies   China pheasant flies up

broad white dogwood bloom
we tried smoking shredded cedarbark

bubbles of pitch in the bark
pull bracken ferns to throw like spears

cows, they
shit as they walk
plop   plop

July–September 2005

53

from *"Writers and the War Against Nature"*

> Soaring just over the sea-foam
> riding the wind of the endless waves
> albatross, out there, way
>
> away,   a far cry
> down from the sky

Winter 2006

What a life!

the single fly
in the spotless Forest Service
campground
toilet

Candle Creek, Oregon

c. September 2007

nine frags

"Don't twist my hair"

Don't twist my hair
old bear

Three-inch teeth
good grief

Vows

The voice (vow)
is a breath (brother),
a spirit, a spiral, a sphere,
it woos (waves—wives,)

the wild

White Rumps

Northern flickers

Pronghorns

Dwarf stars

Receding.

Out West

There's all the time in the universe,

And plenty of wide open space

Country & Western

Loving, hurting,

Cheating, flirting,

Drinking, lying,

Laughing, crying

songs.

(seen on the side of a bus in Louisville Kentucky
April '83. Station WINN)

A buzzy huddle

of shiny flies on the trail

Ah, twisty carcass of a worm.

in Hokkaido

Doctors will be Protected

"Write down" I said to the child who was writing
what I told her,

"That from the notch

carved on the vine between the maple and the
flowering peach,

along the trail and the whole way down to here,

Doctors will be protected. By us."

As I knelt and carved the notch.

Minutes

He wears his warm wig an hour
And mountains of minutes
press his feet between his skull

IAMBICS

The tautology:
  I AM THAT I AM

The paradox:
  I AM NOT THAT   I AM

The practice
  NOT

The fruit
  NOT I   I AM

          July–August 2009

The Dancer Is a Weaver

Her dance is   daily life   transformed

holding a spinner's spindle
face a calm still mask
wheeling slow as the night sky

kimono plain and perfect   robe of dawn
dressed for work
in heaven   in deva space
spindle in hand

moving like the moon   reflecting
brief like   craft   long time

eyes down   face pure   slow

as she goes

Taira Mari's Ryukyu Court Dance performance
Naha, Okinawa, 4.III.2003
2010

The Gooosenecks of the San Juan

The gooosenecks of the San Juan
river   turn, turn, and turn again
this old meander
is entrenched.
500 feet down
in the rock   cliffs,
float and look up at the sky
past   stars   murmuring

—"there you are"—and
"we are here"

2010

Where

Shoot an arrow into the
secret heart of the monster
I once said. But the Airports
Skyscrapers   Markets had no secrets
just more places that won't die.

No use shooting there—

Seek the *secret heart.*
The core, the center, of the monster's power
—not where you thought. It's elsewhere,
hidden in a harmless-looking spot

If you've wiped somebody's nose,
untied a knot, looked for a lost key
maybe a little bird
or mouse   will point
and   whisper in your ear,

shoot there

July 3, 2018

Victoria Falls and Zimbabwe

In 1993 my older son Kai was contracted with the World Wildlife Fund to do GIS mapping of elephant habitat in Zambia. In time he continued this work in Botswana and Zimbabwe. Spring of 1994 my other son Gen and I decided to visit him, and we found ourselves in the northerly town of Maun in Botswana. Maun is at the edge of the big network of wetlands and waterways known as the Okavango marshes—fed by the Chobe River. It hosts a huge population of African wildlife including what is probably the largest herd of wild free-ranging elephants in the world. Kai borrowed an elderly Toyota Land Cruiser and with very little gear and rudimentary maps, we packed up and drove across to Zimbabwe, to the big town of Victoria Falls. This is right at the edge of the Zambezi River, which is the northern boundary of Zimbabwe and Botswana. South of the Zambezi it is known as "Southern Africa" with the nation of South Africa at the bottom of the continent. Victoria Falls (in the days when Zimbabwe was called "Rhodesia" and Brits ran the show) was a very classy tourist town, with its elegant Victoria Falls Hotel.

Today it is a bit run down. Young European backpackers with shaved heads (to avoid lice, they say) make it feel a bit like Kathmandu. One of the marvels of the world, the sublime Victoria Falls, is just down the hill. It is known as "Mosi oa Tunya"—"Smoke that Thunders."

I walk back the half-mile or so out of the park around Victoria Falls and decide "unfinished"—did it too fast—need another trip to the place where it roars, so go down there again.

The Zambezi River (which is huge) comes in a broad sweep, approaches this edge of basalt, lays itself across some ancient volcanic flow, shallows and stretches out on the tableland to a mile wide then drops abruptly over the system of ledges to fall anywhere from 300 to 360 feet down, along that face.

It spills into a narrow channel that runs at right angles to the direction of the falls-flow; it hits a trough and cuts sharp north in a great turmoil. Finally makes a complete sharp bend, turns south again, and from the map (I couldn't see this all on foot) I see it makes another sharp U-bend, turns north. After a few more turns and curves becomes at last a channel—and flows on toward the Indian Ocean.

One walks from the south end out along the first tongue of the table land opposite the falls so you can look right across at falling water, only a few hundred feet from you, the whole way. As one goes farther out the cool moist air wells up in one's face, misting through the increasingly thicker canopy and undergrowth, and then as you step out at a viewing point, you get hit by a blast of cloud and spray and a sight of a perpetual rainbow.

There's first one great cataract coming down, then north a little, a kind of island juts out with some falls dropping off behind that, and this "island" has forest on it with cliffs and water on all sides and then another broad stretch of falls with a great flow first and then a thinner flow over a rocky jumble, then an increased flow again, then another small point of dry land and then another very long arc of breaking water going directly over it and down.

I make my way, point by point, out to the far end, taking my shirt off and putting it in my pack as I am getting drenched now, and the few other tourists walking this far out, black and white alike, are also drenched. Two white girls in high-thigh bathing suits looking totally un-African in their bareness—but I know they'll put on clothes again as soon as they get back towards the entrance. And finally I'm approaching the last rock point where the rising water of the falls is falling in a heavy drenching rain back down on us. The path is awash with a constant flow of inch-deep water flooding back out, sideways over to the edge. The grass here is a marsh and the rocks are covered with moss. The drenching downpour comes in pulses as do waves of mist rising up.

I find myself standing in a cloud of spray and—shades of the penitential warrior priest Mongaku—chanting the Fudo mantra, doing the Yamabushi waterfall practice (hands in gassho, standing straight in the cold downpour, meditating in the midst of the downpour, eyes closed. For days and days—the meeting of the ceaseless flow and stubborn hardness—)

And the energy-package all this represents—volcanism, tectonics, subduction and the globe, the planetary "heat engine" that makes the cycles of weather and water.

Finally, sopping, I'm looking over the edge at the very far point of this, half off the cliff, hanging onto a share of a piece of a boulder, I can see straight down into the whirling, frothing channels below. I recall my Yamabushi teacher saying as he hung me over the cliffs of Mt. Omine (in Japan) "just tell the truth." Reticulate foam shows up in a quick shaft of sunlight between the mist—huge raindrops falling, while between and through them, fine mist is rising, all at the same time. The natural magic of the planet.

And walk back beyond the reach of the heavy rains, only a few hundred yards away by path and it gets much drier. Take off my canvas shorts and wring them out and then walk slowly back up trail again, listening to the roar, touching from time to time on mist.

I've seen a mother and daughter, 11-year-old girl, the daughter in swimming suit who is ecstatically jumping up and down, waving her arms, getting wet—thoroughly taken by the whole scene, at the junction of the trails, see the ecstatic look on the little face.

She's still doing jumping jacks and waving her arms and rubbing the water on her skin and on her chest. I say to the mother, "This is a place you can't stay dry, isn't it. I was here yesterday and I couldn't help but come back again." And she laughs, and speaks (an American accent), "Well we were here this morning and did all of this one time and my daughter insisted we come back again."

As I walk back toward the gate, note the gradual change in vegetation away from the almost cloud forest that has formed along the lip where the spray rises from the Falls into the more common acrid crackly dry leaves on the ground, trees, and bushes. Trees: red-leaf fig and *Acacia galpinii*, with big vines on it. By the time I get to the gate my chest has already dried off, my hair is half dry, I put my t-shirt back on. In wet shorts and dry t-shirt, little day pack, walk back up by trail taking the Victoria Falls Hotel branch, a trail spattered by elephant droppings. And ran into an elephant! Close, also out for a walk.

Go through the backside of the old colonial Victoria Falls Hotel with its broad clipped lawn, its starched waiters, its patio laid out for tea or dinner, and pass right through the lobby and reception room in a décor of white and light green and on down the steps to the limousine stop, and down the gated driveway of the Hotel to the broad half-dirt main street that runs between town proper and the waterfalls. Head for our tent-site out in the public camping-ground. A continuous stream of variously-dressed people, walking, walking, everywhere. No whites.

Zimbabwe 1994
c. 2016–20

By the Chobe River

Botswana. Zambia border

The new moon crescent settles in a lavender dusk

An elephant shadow slides beyond the rise

Bathing by a faucet with a bucket,

sitting on a shattered concrete block

The old Landcruiser engine cooling

Just before hyenas come.

c. 2016–20

For Robert Duncan

Walking down Grant Street just short of the Place
    late at night
ran into Robert Duncan, we embraced,
    nineteen fifty five.
        He said, "Gary your number."
Gave me a copy
of *Letters*; signed it standing in the streetlight.
number 69. The gleam
in Robert's sidelong eye

    And I think of Neuri,
whose elbows and jaw-juts and knees all jangling
I wrapped up in my arms and packed into the car,
'37 Packard,
her so drunk, she beat my
face and eye—mean and sweet—
and in the poem I wrote for her I said
"because I once beat you up"
when it was me got whacked.
    Old "male chivalry"
and a literary scholar trots it out
    because I'm "Allen's friend"
slender girl I never slept with
you liked women.

And I loved Robert for his teaching
Some crime.

c. 2016–20

Song for Wrecked Cars

cars   wrecked, washed
strewn through the desert,
trash   space
            ironwood limbs lit by the moon
            mesquite twig   breeze
cars
rusting to death
while alive

c. 2016–20

After Dōgen

Mimulus on the cliffside in April
Nuthatches in the summer pines
Cranes calling south in September
Winter pond-ice crackling bright

c. 2016–20

Having Seen on Earth

The Taj Mahal, cool marble upward space, a uterine
emptiness edged
    with tracework, for the love of Mumtaz Mahal

Nanda Devi appearing from behind the cloud, as we stood under
blossoming
    rhododendron at Kausani, in Almora

The Zambezi river topple and crash, Victoria Falls,
    soaked in spray

The Southern Cross in the night—through tangled hair—from under a
    woman on a beach in Samoa

The Buddha's seat at Bodh Gaya still shaded by a giant Fig

The Temple of the Sixth Patriarch of Zen, Hui-Neng, in Guangzhou
city, well-
    kept but now an "educational park" with a picture of him splitting
wood

The complex Lama Temple in Beijing, being repainted and touched up
by art
    students from the University

The six great snowpeaks of the Northwest—all Koma
Kulshan, Tahoma, Klickitat, Loowit, Shuksan,
    Wyeast
    above the clouds at dawn

Looking into the lava cauldron of Smoking Island, Ten Islands
Archipelago,
    East China Sea

A huge shark's shadow passing over, as I spearfished deep
in the green water
    alone off the reef of Suwa-no-se Island

An elephant black and shining, bathing in a pool in the Chobe
savannah—
    water streaming off her as she rose.

c. 2016–20

Bai Juyi's "Long Bitter Song"

The "Long Bitter Song" ("Chang hen ge") of Bai Juyi (Po Chü-I) is probably the best known and most widely popular poem in the whole Chinese cultural-sphere. Bai and his friend Wang Shifu (Wang Shih-fu) were visiting the Xienfu Chan Buddhist training center in 806, and were talking one night of the events of the reign of Emperor Xuanzong (Hsüan Tsung) and the An Lushan rebellion, sixty years earlier. Xuanzong was one of China's better rulers and presided over what has since been considered the golden age of both Chan Buddhist creativity and Chinese poetry. He took power in 712 and led a strong and innovative administration up to about 745. At that time he became totally infatuated with Yang Gui Fei (Yang Kuei-fei), the wife of one of his many sons. She became his concubine, the Sogdian-Turkish general An Lushan became an intimate of the couple and perhaps also a lover of Yang, the restive Northeast revolted under An, he led his troops into the capital, Xuanzong, Yang Gui Fei and the palace guard fled the city, and outside town at Horse Cliff the troops stopped, refused to go on, and insisted on putting Yang Gui Fei to death. That was in 755. The rebellion was quelled by 762, about the same time Xuanzong died. This rebellion marked a watershed in the fortunes of the Tang dynasty, beginning a period of somewhat more decentralized power, a rise of Chinese cultural chauvinism and contempt for the "third world" border peoples, and a greater weakness in relation to the borders.

The story of the Emperor and his lovely concubine had become legend. After that evening's reminiscences, Bai was inspired to write the story as a long poem. Within his own lifetime he then heard it sung on the canals and in the pleasure quarters by singing-girls and minstrels. Bai lived from A.D. 772 to 846. He was born in a poor family, passed the examinations partly on the strength of his literary brilliance, and became a lifelong political functionary of great integrity and compassion who wrote many stirring poems on behalf of the common people. He was a Chan Buddhist, and studied under the master Wei Kuan, who was a disciple of the outstanding Chan teacher Mazu (Ma-tsu).

This poem is in the seven character line, which gives it (in Chinese) this sort of rhythm:

tum tum / tum tum: tum tum tum

I have tried to keep this beat as far as possible in my translation. I did the first version of it with the aid of Ch'en Shih-hsiang who was my teacher in graduate seminars at U.C. Berkeley in Tang poetics, in the early fifties. I must take full responsibility, however, for idiosyncratic aspects of the translation—cases of both stripped-down literalism, and occasional free flights. My debt to his gracious, learned, unquenchable delight in all forms of poetry is deep indeed, and I am pleased to honor his memory with this publication of a poem that we took much pleasure in reading together.

28.X.86

Long Bitter Song

I

Han's Emperor wanted a Beauty
    one to be a "Destroyer of Kingdoms"
Scouring the country, many years,
    sought, but didn't find.
The Yang family had a girl
    just come grown;
Reared deep in the inner-apartments,
    men didn't know of her.
Such Heaven-given elegance
    could not be concealed
One morning she was taken to
    the Emperor's household.
A turn of the head, one smile,
    —a hundred lusts were flamed
The Six Palaces rouge-and-eyebrow
    without one beautiful face.
In the Spring cold she was given a bath
    at the Flower-pure Pool
Warm pool, smooth water,
    on her cold, glowing skin
Servant girls helping her rise,
    languorous, effortless beauty—
This was the beginning of her new role:
    glistening with Imperial favour.
Hair like a floating cloud, flower-face,
    ripple of gold when she walked.
—In the warm Hibiscus curtains
    they spent the Spring night.
Spring night is bitterly short
    it was noon when they rose;
From this time on the Emperor
    held no early court.

Holding feasts and revels
      without a moment's rest
Spring passed, Spring dalliance,
      all in a whirl of nights.
Beautiful girls in the outer palace:
      three thousand women:
Love enough for three thousand
      centered in one body.
In Gold House, perfectly attired
      her beauty served the night;
In the Jade Tower the parties ended
      with drunk, peaceful Spring.
Here sisters and brothers
      all given land,
Splendor and brilliance
      surprised her humble family.
Following this, on all the earth,
      fathers & mothers hearts
No longer valued bearing males
      but hoped to have girls.
The high-soaring Li palace
      pierces blue clouds
Delights of Immortals, whirled on wind
      were heard of everywhere.
Slow song, flowing dance,
      music like frost-crystal
      sifting from the lute-strings—
The Emperor could exhaust a day
      watching—and still not full

II

Then Yuyang war drums,
      approached, shaking the earth;
Alarming, scattering, the "Rainbow Skirt"
      the "Feathered Robe" dances.
From the nine great City-Towers,
      smoke, dust, rose.
Thousands of chariots, ten thousand horsemen
      scattered Southwest—

Kingfisher banner fluttering, rippling,
        going and then stopping;
West out the city walls
        over a hundred li
And the six armies won't go on:
        nothing can be done—
Writing, twisting, Moth-eyebrows
        dies in front of the horses.
Her flower comb falls to the ground
        not a man will pick it up—
Kingfisher feathers, "little golden birds,"
        jade hair-pin;
The Emperor hides his face
        no way to help
Turns, looks, blood, tears,
        flow, quietly mingle.
Yellow dust eddies and scatters.
        Desolate winds blow.
Cloud Trail winds and twists
        climbing to Sword-point Peak
Under Omei Shan
        the last few came.
Flags, banners, without brightness,
        a meagre-coloured sun.
Shu river waters blue
        Shu mountains green
And the Emperor, days, days,
        nights, nights, brooding.
From the temporary palace, watching the moon
        colour tore his heart
The night-rain bell-tinkle
        —bowel-twisting music.

III

Heaven turns, earth revolves,
        The Dragon-Chariot returned.
But he was irresolute,
        didn't want to go;
And at the foot of Horse Cliff,
        in the sticky mud,

Couldn't find the Jade Face
    at her death-place.
Court officials watching him
    soaked their clothes with tears.
Looking east to the Capital walls,
    they returned on horses
Came back to Pond Park
    —all was as before.
Taiye Hibiscus,
    Weiyang Willow.
But Hibiscus flowers were like her face,
    the Willows like her brow:
Seeing this, how could he
    keep tears from falling.
Spring wind, peach, plum,
    flowers open in the sun;
Autumn rain, Wutong trees,
    leaf-fall time.
Western palace, the inner court,
    many autumn grasses.
Falling leaves fill the stairs
    red: and no one sweeps.
The Pear-garden players
    white-haired young.
Pepper-court eunuchs
    watched beautiful girls age.
Evening, palace, glow-worm flight,
    —his thoughts were soundless.
He picked his single candle-wick down,
    couldn't reach sleep.
Slow, slow, the night bell
    begins the long night,
Glimmering, fading, the Milky Way,
    and day about to dawn.
Silent tile roof-ducks
    are heavy with frost-flowers
The Kingfisher quilt is cold—
    who will share his bed?
Far, far, the living and the dead
    and the light years—cut apart.

Her spirit already dissolving,
    not even entering dreams.

IV

A Linqiong Daoist priest
    of the Hongdu school
Was able to deeply concentrate
    and thus call up the spirits.
Hearing this, the Emperor
    —troubled, twisting thoughts.
Ordered the Daoist priest
    to make a thorough search.
Pushing the sky, riding air,
    swift as a thunderbolt,
Harrowing the heavens, piercing Earth,
    he sought everywhere
Above exhausting the blue void,
    below, the Yellow Springs.
The ends of earth—vast, vast,
    and nowhere did he find her.
Then he heard—that out on the ocean—
    was a mountain of Immortals
A mountain at—nowhere—
    a cloudy, unreal place.
Palace towers, tinkling gems,
    where Five Clouds rise.
Within—lovely, wanton, chaste,
    many faery people.
There was there one faery
    called Taizhen;
Snow skin, flower appearance,
    it had to be her.
At the Gold Tower of the West Wing,
    he knocked on the Jade door:
Announcing himself to Little Jade
    —and she told Shuang Cheng,
That the Emperor of the people of Han
    had sent an envoy.

In the nine-flowered canopy
	the faery's dreams were broken;
Holding her clothes, pushing the pillow,
	she rose, walking unsteady.
Winding, opening the pearl door,
	the inlaid silver screens.
Her cloud-like hair, floating on one side,
	—just brought from sleep.
Her flower-cap unadjusted
	she came down the hall,
Wind blew her elegant sleeves
	floating, floating up—
Seemed like the "Rainbow Skirt,"
	the "Feathered Robe" dance.
Her jade-like figure small and alone,
	she scattered her sad tears:
As though one branch of a blossoming pear
	was holding the whole Spring's rain.
Restraining her feelings, cooling her look,
	she told him to thank the Emperor;
"With that parting our two forms
	were split by the World's vast shifting;
After Zhaoyang temple,
	our love was cut off.
Here in Raspberry-tangle Palace
	the days and months are long—
I look down, hoping to see
	lands where humans dwell,
I never see Chang'an
	but only dusty haze."
Then taking some ancient treasures
	rich in deep feeling,
An inlaid box, a gold hairpin,
	to be delivered back,
Keeping a leg of the hairpin,
	keeping half the box,
Breaking the gold of the hairpin,
	box cut in two—
"If only our hearts are strong as
	this gold hairpin,

Above in heaven, or among men,
      we will somehow meet.
Go back swiftly
      tell him this message:
For it tells of one Vow
      that two hearts know,
In the seventh month on the seventh day
      in Long-Life Temple.
At midnight, no one about,
      we swore together
If in heaven, to fly as
      the 'paired-wing' birds;
If on earth, to grow as
      one joined branch."
Heaven lasts, Earth endures,
      —and both will end;
This sorrow stretches on
      forever, without limit.

Sixteen T'ang Poems

Note for Sixteen T'ang Poems

In the early fifties I managed to get myself accepted into the Department of Oriental Languages at UC Berkeley as a graduate student. I took seminars in the reading of T'ang and Sung poems with Professor Ch'en Shih-hsiang, a remarkable scholar, calligrapher, poet, and critic who had a profound appreciation for good poetry of any provenance. Ch'en Shih-hsiang introduced me to the Han-shan poems, and I published those translations back in the sixties. The poems translated here also got their start in those seminars, but I never considered them quite finished. From Berkeley I went to Japan and for the subsequent decade was working almost exclusively with Ch'an texts. Another twenty years went into developing a farmstead in the Sierra Nevada and working for the ecological movement. In the last few years I have had a chance to return to my readings in Chinese poetry and bring a few of the poems I started back then to completion. This little collection is dedicated to the memory of Ch'en Shih-hsiang.

14.1.93

Two Poems by Meng Hao-jan

Spring Dawn

Spring sleep, not yet awake to dawn,
I am full of birdsongs.
Throughout the night the sounds of wind and rain
Who knows   what flowers fell.

Mooring on Chien-te River

The boat rocks at anchor by the misty island
Sunset, my loneliness comes again.
In these vast wilds the sky arches down to the trees,
In the clear river water, the moon draws near.

Five Poems by Wang Wei

DEER CAMP

Empty mountains:
    no one to be seen.
Yet—hear—
      human sounds and echoes.
    Returning sunlight
    enters the dark woods;
Again shining
    on green moss, above.

BAMBOO LANE HOUSE

Sitting alone, hid in bamboo
Plucking the lute and gravely whistling.
People wouldn't know that deep woods
Can be this bright   in the moon.

SAYING FAREWELL

Me in the mountains   and now you've left.
Sunset,   I close the peephole door.
Next spring   when grass is green,
Will you   return once more?

THINKING OF US

Red beans grow in the south
In spring they put out shoots.
Gather a lapful for me—
And doing it, think of us.

POEM

You who come from my village
Ought to know its affairs
The day you passed the silk window
Had the chill plum bloomed?

Three Poems for Women in the Service of the Palace

AUTUMN EVENING
Tu Mu

A silver candle in the autumn gloom
    by a lone painted screen
Her small light gauze fan
    shivers the fireflies
On the stairs of heaven, night's color
    cool as water;
She sits watching the Herd-boy,
    the Weaving-girl, stars.

The Herd-boy is Altair, in Aquila.
The Weaving-girl in Vega, in Lyra.

THE SUMMER PALACE
Yuan Chen

Silence settles on the old Summer Palace
Palace flowers   still   quiet   red.
White-haired concubines
Idly sit and gossip   of the days of Hsüan Tsung.

PALACE SONG
Po Chü-i

Tears soak her thin shawl
    dreams won't come.
In the dark night, from the front palace,
    girls rehearsing songs.
Still fresh and young,
    already put down,
She leans across the brazier
    to wait the coming dawn.

Spring View
Tu Fu

The nation is ruined,   but mountains and rivers remain.
This spring the city   is deep in weeds and brush.
Touched by the times   even flowers weep tears,
Fearing leaving   the birds tangled hearts.
Watch-tower fires   have been burning for three months
To get a note from home   would cost ten thousand gold.
Scratching my   white hair thinner
Seething hopes   all in a trembling hairpin.

Events of the An Lushan rebellion.

Parting from Ling Ch'e

Liu Ch'ang-ch'ing

Green, green
      bamboo-grove temple
Dark, dark,
      the bell-sounding evening.
His rainhat catches
      the slanting sunlight,
Alone returning
      from the distant blue peaks.

Climbing Crane Tower
Wang Chih-huan

The white sun has gone over the mountains
The yellow river is flowing to the sea.
If you wish to see a thousand *li*
Climb one story higher in the tower.

River Snow

Lo Tsung-yuan

These thousand peaks cut off the flight of birds
On all the trails, human tracks are gone.
A single boat—coat—hat—an old man!
Alone   fishing   chill   river   snow.

Parting with Hsin Chien at Hibiscus Tavern
Wang Ch'ang-ling

Cold rain on the river
  we enter Wu by night
At dawn I leave
  for Ch'u-shan, alone.
If friends in Lo-yang
  ask after me, I've
"A heart like ice
  in a jade vase."

Two Poems Written at Maple Bridge
Near Su-chou

Maple Bridge Night Mooring
Chang Chi

Moon set, a crow caws,
    frost fills the sky
River, maple, fishing-fires
    cross my troubled sleep.
Beyond the walls of Su-chou
    from Cold Mountain temple
The midnight bell sounds
    reach my boat.

(circa 765 AD)

At Maple Bridge
Gary Snyder

Men are mixing gravel and cement
At Maple bridge,
Down an alley by a tea-stall
From Cold Mountain temple;
Where Chang Chi heard the bell.
The stone step moorage
Empty, lapping water,
And the bell sound has travelled
Far across the sea.

1984 AD

GARY SNYDER is the author of more than twenty collections of poetry and prose. Since 1970, he has lived in the watershed of the South Yuba River in the foothills of the Sierra Nevada. Winner of the Pulitzer Prize in 1975, Snyder has also been awarded the Bollingen Prize for Poetry and the Robert Kirsch Award for lifetime achievement. His 1992 collection, *No Nature*, was a National Book Award finalist, and in 2008 he received the Ruth Lilly Poetry Prize. Snyder is a poet, environmentalist, educator, and Zen Buddhist.